Wondrous World

of the  Mangrove Swamps

of Florida, Bahamas, Turks and Caicos, and Caribbean

by Katherine Orr

Acknowledgments

My thanks to the many individuals who dedicate their lives to the study and understanding of nature, and to those who bring this knowledge to the world.

WONDROUS WORLD OF THE MANGROVE SWAMPS
  of Florida, Bahamas, Turks and Caicos, and Caribbean

Written and illustrated by Katherine Orr
Designed by Angela Wix

First edition published in 1989 by Florida Flair Books
Second edition publihed in 2021 by NATUREBOOKS

Copyright © 2021 by Katherine Orr
ISBN: 978-1-7354042-4-0
All rights reserved. Portions of this book may be reproduced and modified for educationl purposes with permission from the author. For quetions and permissions contact Katherine Orr at katherineshelleyorr.com

Printed in the United States of America

Contents

Acknowledgments ii	Above Water 15
Journey into Mystery 1	Below Water 17
Salt Water Trees 3	Shoreline Protector 19
The Red Mangrove 4	Nurseries and Nutrients 21
Life Cycle 6	The Magic Cycle 23
Land Stabilizer 9	Mangroves in Danger 25
Other Mangroves 11	Destruction 26
Mangroves of the World........... 12	The Future 27
A Refuge for Wildlife: Everglades National Park 13	Journey's End 28

Journey into Mystery

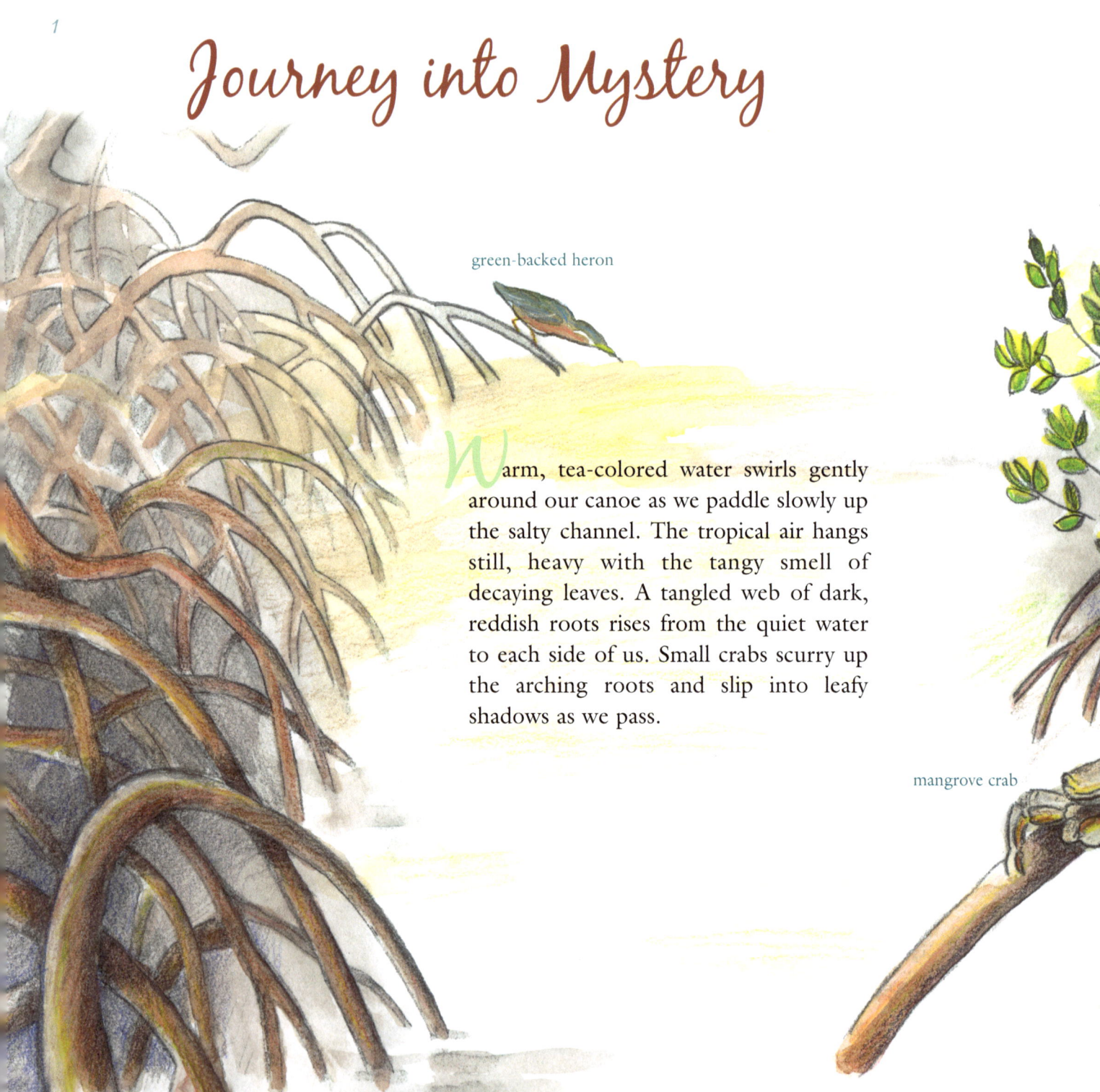

green-backed heron

Warm, tea-colored water swirls gently around our canoe as we paddle slowly up the salty channel. The tropical air hangs still, heavy with the tangy smell of decaying leaves. A tangled web of dark, reddish roots rises from the quiet water to each side of us. Small crabs scurry up the arching roots and slip into leafy shadows as we pass.

mangrove crab

Up ahead, a green-backed heron stands poised on a mangrove root, ready to stab at a careless minnow with her dagger-sharp beak. As we draw closer, she gives a loud "kaank" of alarm and takes flight. On silent wings she vanishes around a bend up ahead.

From a distance, the mangrove shore looks like a solid wall of greenery, but the broad, flat swamp is penetrated by countless open channels and narrow creeks. Now, one such winding watery trail is taking us through the heart of the mangrove forest to explore its mysteries. What are mangrove trees? How do they live and why are they important? We have come to find out.

Salt Water Trees

Mangroves are a diverse but relatively limited collection of trees. They are not all closely related, yet all share the ability to grow in salty, swampy, tropical environments. More than fifty species of mangrove live in tropical and subtropical climates throughout the world. They grow in wet soil that is periodically or permanently submerged by flooding from rivers or tides, and they can withstand salty conditions that would kill most plants. To live in this salty world, mangroves have developed ingenious methods of keeping excess salt from their systems. Some block salt intake at the roots; some excrete it from their leaves; some have the added ability to store salt in leaves that are then dropped from the tree.

Although mangroves grow well in fresh water, most do not compete well with other freshwater plants for nutrients, light, and space. Only along salty shores where land and sea meet, where fresh and salt waters mix, do mangroves create vast, swampy forests. They have claimed the saltwater environment for their own.

The Red Mangrove

The trees that surround us as we paddle up the channel are red mangroves. The red mangrove, called *Rhizophora mangle* by scientists, is the most common and distinctive mangrove in Florida, the Bahamas, the Turks and Caicos Islands and the Caribbean. It is easily recognized by its high, stilt-like prop roots. These arching roots spread outward from the main trunk in all directions and hold the tree upright in the soft mud. Aerial roots drop down from the branches to lend additional support and to help hold the tree steady, even in hurricane winds. As we look closely, we notice small, pale "breathing pores" called *lenticels* scattered along the roots. These lenticels exchange gases with the surrounding air.

We reach for a low branch and examine the leaves. They are tough and rather glossy. These sturdy leaves, with their slightly waxy surface, help the tree retain moisture. Although most of the leaves are dark green, some are yellow and ready to fall. The mangrove does not drop all its leaves at once, but sheds them gradually throughout the year. In this way it remains green throughout the seasons, even though new leaves are produced each year. This steady rain of leaves plays an important role in the marine environment, as we shall see later.

Life Cycle

One must look closely to see the small yellow flowers of the red mangrove blooming near the tip of the branch. By contrast, the large dart-shaped "seedlings" that dangle like giant green beans are impossible to miss. Unlike most trees, red mangrove flowers produce fruits that do not contain true seeds. Instead, the fruit develops directly into a young plant while still attached to the parent tree. What looks like a long bean hanging from the red mangrove's branch is really a young offspring, or *propagule*.

propagule

These bronze-tipped propagules may grow more than sixteen inches (forty centimeters) long before they fall from the tree. Although mangroves can flower throughout the year, most red mangroves flower in late spring and summer, and drop their propagules in the summer and autumn of the following year.

When a propagule falls, it may penetrate soft mud beneath the parent tree and anchor immediately, or it may fall into the water and drift away. A red mangrove propagule can remain alive for up to one year, while waves and water currents carry it far from where it fell. At first, the propagule floats horizontally. As it becomes waterlogged, its tip sinks, bringing it to a vertical position. If all goes well, the propagule drifts to a sheltered area and lodges upright among shells or other debris in shallow water, near the high tide line. Then tiny new roots sprout from the tip of the propagule, anchoring it in its new home. A spindly stem, topped by fresh green leaves, shoots skyward. A new mangrove tree has arrived.

a fallen propagule may anchor immediately beneath the parent tree

or it may be carried away to a new location

Land Stabilizer

black skimmer

The young red mangrove tree sends out its first arching prop roots when it is about two years old. As the tree grows taller and fuller, it produces more prop roots. Slowly, new prop roots spread outward in all directions, forming a tangled maze that holds the tree securely in the wet mud. As other propagules anchor and grow nearby, a new mangrove colony is established. A dense network of prop roots spreads over the watery landscape like a tangled web of interlacing fingers, holding the sand and mud in place and stabilizing the land. Soil, leaves, twigs, and other debris collect among the roots. These pile up and pack together over time, compacting the soft mud and helping to create firm ground.

Although mangroves have been called land builders, this can be misleading because mngroves settle in areas where sediments are already accumulating; they help the land-building process, rather than control it. We live at a time when the

loggerhead sea turtle

earth's sea level is rising. In most places, the sea level is rising as fast or faster than the rate at which mangroves can build higher land, so the best mangroves can do is to help maintain our shorelines against the encroaching sea.

Changes in water currents can erode away mangrove shoreline quite quickly. Mangroves cannot spread into areas with strong currents, nor can they spread their forests into places that are not already wetlands. The physical water characteristics of an area — waves, currents, tides, and water drainage from land — as well as major storms, control the growth of mangrove swamps. A healthy swamp is in balance with its environment. Should the water environment change dramatically, the mangroves in that area would probably die.

Other Mangroves

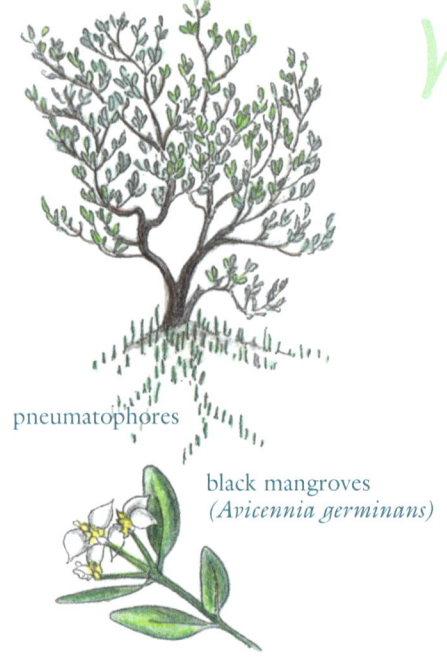

pneumatophores

black mangroves
(*Avicennia germinans*)

white mangrove
(*Laguncularia racemosa*)

We slide our canoe onto a mud bank and carefully step ashore. Here we find trees with dark, twisted limbs. The soft ground around their trunks is covered with pencil-sized projections poking up from the earth like pointing fingers. These trees are black mangroves (*Avicennia germinans*) and the spiky projections are special "breathing roots" called *pneumatophores* (noo-MAT-o-forz).

A normal function of tree roots is to exchange gases with the surrounding soil. Wet swamp mud, unlike drier soil, lacks air circulating through it, so mangroves have developed their own ways to get around this problem. Black mangroves extend long, shallow roots horizontally beneath the mud. Pneumatophores project upward along these roots, reaching needed air and avoiding toxins accumulated in the mud. Small lenticels on the pneumatophores are the sites at which the roots exchange gases with the surrounding air.

We spy the oval leaves of a white mangrove (*Laguncularia racemosa*) growing along the water. Unlike red and black mangroves, the white mangrove rarely grows directly in the water, and so rarely needs special roots to cope with the airless soil. This white mangrove, however, has several small breathing roots whose odd, knobby shapes remind us of wooden toadstools in an elfin forest.

buttonwood
(*Conocarpus erecta*)

As we approach a small hummock, we find several buttonwood trees (*Conocarpus erecta*) sharing the higher ground. Buttonwoods are sometimes regarded as the fourth mangrove in our area because they are related to the white mangrove and are commonly found rimming the upland edges of the swamp. Yet, unlike the other three mangroves, buttonwood is not very tolerant of flooding and grows extensively in seaside environments other than mangrove swamps.

Mangroves Around the World

Mangrove swamps occur along seacoasts in warm climates around the world. They grow in sheltered areas where land meets sea, including estuaries, lagoons, and tidal creeks. They commonly form swampy forests that fringe the coasts of bays, islands, and the mouths of rivers where the land is periodically flooded by high tides or rivers swollen from rain. Soil nutrients wash from the land and nourish the trees. If the flooded area is very broad and includes fresh water, such as in river deltas and flood plains, the swamp may cover a vast area, with trees reaching sixty to one hundred feet high. In parts of Asia, forests of giant mangroves span many hundreds of square miles. By contrast, dwarf mangroves grow in places where their roots are constricted by hard limestone ground, and where the trees are stressed by too much salt or cold. Dwarf mangrove swamps are common among dry, limestone islands, such as The Bahamas, the Turks and Caicos Islands, and the Florida Keys. The trees in some of these swamps may never reach five feet high.

A Refuge for Wildlife:
Everglades National Park

double-crested cormorant

TAKE ONLY PICTURES
LEAVE ONLY FOOTPRINTS

alligator

In southwestern Florida lies one of the largest mangrove forests in the Western hemisphere, part of which is contained within the vast tract of Everglades National Park. Every year, thousands of tourists come to the Everglades to experience nature and to view some of the wildlife that lives there. They come to the mangrove creeks and bays, where saltwater merges with fresh, to watch elegant wading birds, such as tricolored herons, snowy egrets and roseate spoonbills. Here, they are almost sure to see the double-crested cormorant drying its spreading wings in the sun, and an alligator lying motionless, like a thick log along a muddy bank. If they are lucky, they will glimpse a mother manatee guiding her calf through a mangrove-lined waterway. And if they come in the spring, visitors will hear eerie roars ringing through the swamp as a male alligator bellows his gritty love song and is anwered by a female.

great white heron surveying a flock of roseate spoonbills

Twelve endangered species live within the park. At least seven of these — including two kinds of sea turtle, the American crocodile, and the gentle manatee — inhabit the mangrove swamps. It is no wonder that Everglades National Park has been declared a World Heritage Site by the United Nations. Also a biosphere reserve, the park is one of only eight places in the world to have this dual designation. Truly, North America's only subtropical wilderness is a place to be cherished. For here people can still take time to listen, be alone, and feel the spirit of nature that runs through all life.

mangrove cuckoo

white pelicans in flight

Above Water

We paddle quietly, hoping to glimpse some of the many animals that live here. The smooth, reddish prop roots near our boat are spotted with brown mangrove snails and white barnacles. The snails hang quietly on the shaded side of the roots, above water. Unlike true marine snails, they will drown if they remain submerged for too long. Multi-colored crabs scurry along the roots, feeding on plants and fallen leaves. Along the muddy banks, fiddler crabs watch cautiously from their burrows as we glide by. A mud turtle has crawled onto an old log to sun itself. It plunges into the water as we pass, sliding across a set of footprints left by an opossum.

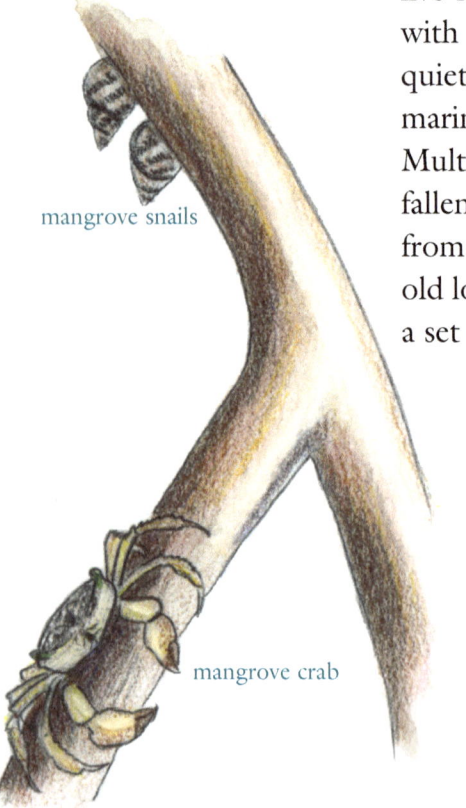
mangrove snails

mangrove crab

fiddler crab

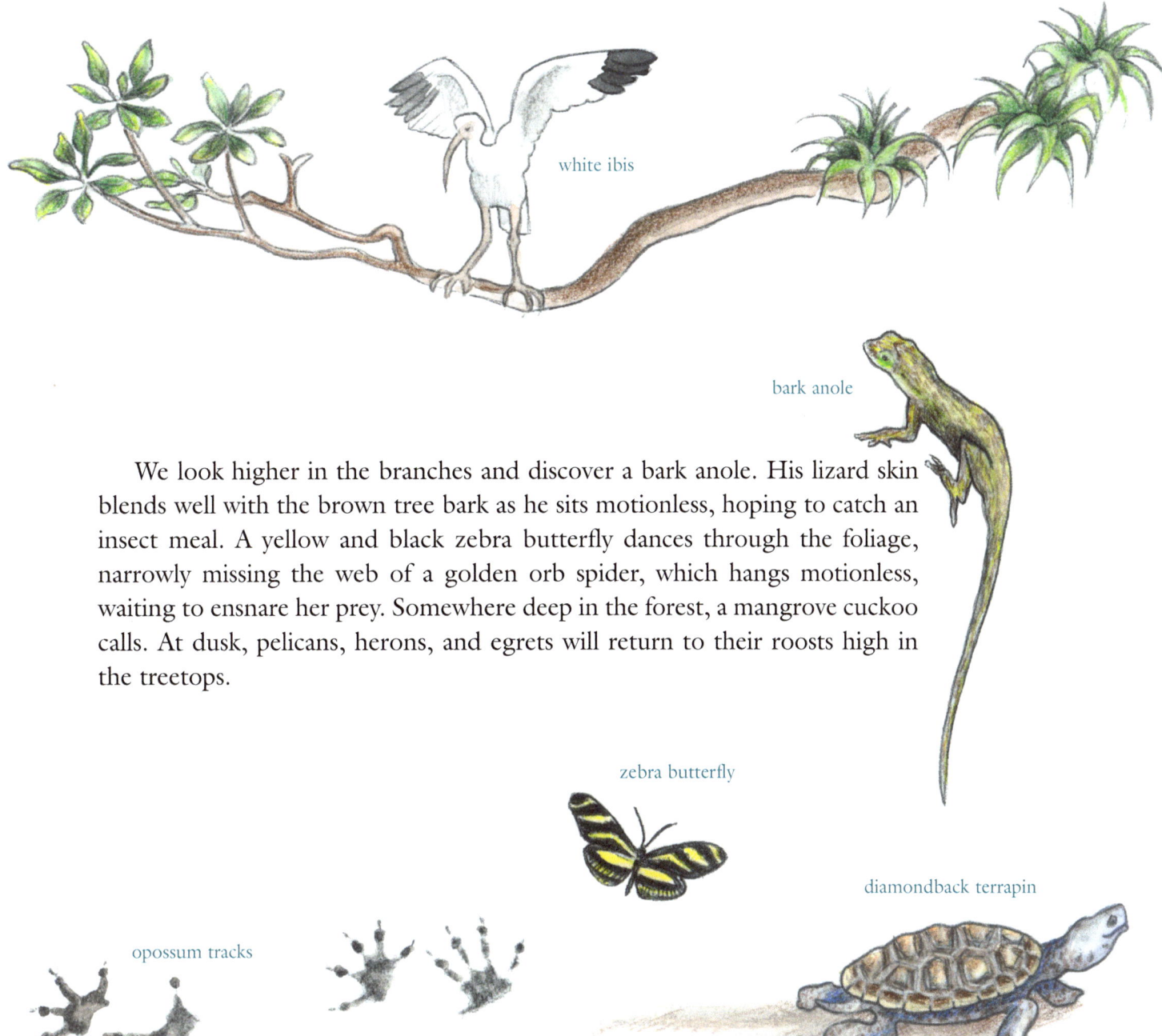

We look higher in the branches and discover a bark anole. His lizard skin blends well with the brown tree bark as he sits motionless, hoping to catch an insect meal. A yellow and black zebra butterfly dances through the foliage, narrowly missing the web of a golden orb spider, which hangs motionless, waiting to ensnare her prey. Somewhere deep in the forest, a mangrove cuckoo calls. At dusk, pelicans, herons, and egrets will return to their roosts high in the treetops.

Below Water

foureye butterflyfish

mullet

rock beauty

juvenile gray angelfish among sabellid worms

We pull on our facemasks and slide over the side of our canoe into the warm water. We are now floating in a world of honey-brown light and shadow. Young schoolmaster snappers glide silently among the dense prop root forest. A school of silvery mullet darts past us in the channel, while a rock beauty and two butterfly fish slip in and out of the shadows.

The submerged prop roots, so smooth above water, now are wrapped in furry coats of growth. Green plumes mingle with tiny green parasols, swaying gracefully on slim stems. These are but two of the many underwater plants called *algae* (AL-jee).

Flat, black tree oysters clump along the roots at the water line. Below them, feathery hydroids and tube worms cluster among orange and brown sponges. Baby lobsters and brittle stars, fairy shrimps and fireworms, sponge crabs and sea slugs, anemones and arrow crabs are some of the many animals that live among the roots.

We hear the popping sounds of hidden snapping shrimp and the crunching of feeding fish. Even on the muddy bottom there is life: strands of algae bearing clusters of tiny green balls trail across the mud. Several *Cassiopea* jellyfish sit upside down, pulsing quietly.

Shoreline Protector

The tsunami that hit Indonesia in 2004 killed thousands of people and caused great damage to homes and buildings, tourism, commercial infrastructure, farmlands and agriculture. Had mangrove swamps been preserved in these regions, the devastation would have been vastly reduced and many lives saved. This tragic experience brings an opportunity for increased awareness about the enormous value of mangroves.

Fishermen and sailors around the world take their boats deep into mangrove swamps when a bad storm threatens. They know that mangrove swamps afford better protection from waves and wind than any other coastal area. The dense network of roots and branches breaks up the force of wind, storm waves and tsumanis, helping to absorb their destructive impact.

Every day, mangrove swamps protect our shores from erosion by reducing the loss of soil nutrients that are washed from the land by rain and rivers. Their tangled roots act as a net or filter, trapping silt and soil in the swamp, where its nutrients are recycled. This filtering action has a second benefit: it helps keep our coastal seas clear and clean. Many forms of marine life, including coral reefs, are killed by cloudy, silt-filled water. For many coral reefs, the filtering action of mangrove swamps spells the difference between life and death.

Nurseries and Nutrients

Of the mangrove swamp's many roles, none is more important than its role as a nursery and food source for marine life. Warm, quiet waters and dense forests of prop roots provide abundant food and shelter for many marine animals. Some of these are babies that will move out to the coral reefs and shallow sea as they grow older and larger. Others will spend their lives in the mangroves, providing valuable food for bigger animals. Still other animals that don't live in the mangroves use them as feeding grounds and places to bear their young.

juvenile jackknife

juvenile barracuda

juvenile spiny lobster

juvenile grunts

juvenile rock beauty

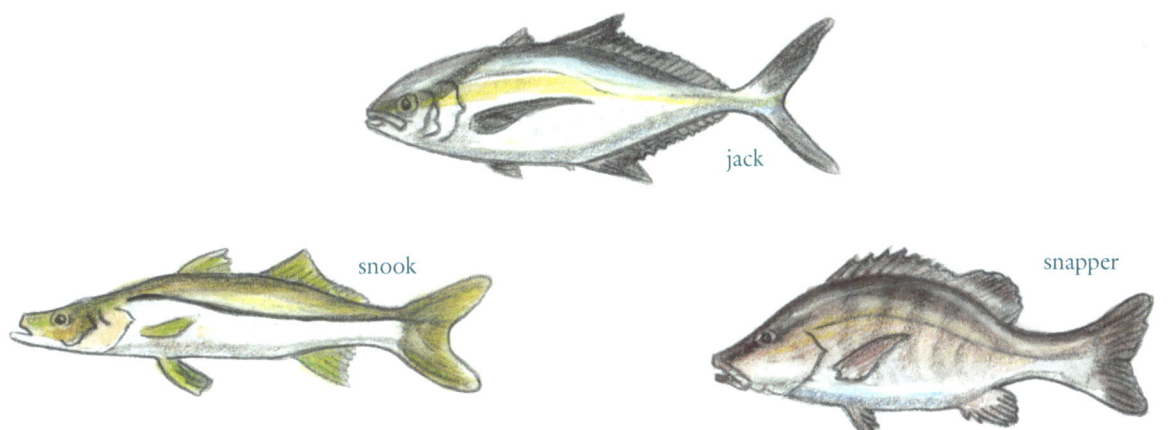

It is astonishing to realize that most of the sport fish, food fish, and shellfish captured off our tropical seacoasts — such as snappers, snooks, mullet, tarpon, sea trout, jacks, pink shrimp, spiny lobsters, sheepshead, and oysters — depend on the mangrove as a nursery or feeding ground for at least part of their lives. Even some fish and shellfish that never visit the mangroves depend on them for food. The secret of how mangroves nourish so many kinds of marine life begins with the mangrove leaf….

The Magic Cycle

When a mangrove leaf falls from the tree into the water, it begins a journey in which its nutrients are passed on to marine life throughout our coastal seas. First, tiny microbes, such as bacteria, protozoans and fungi, slowly decompose the leaf. As microbes feed on the mangrove leaf, it gradually disintegrates into thousands of small particles, each coated with millions of feeding microbes. Small animals, such as shrimp and worms, eat the microbes and are nourished by them. Other larger animals eat the shrimp and worms, and are nourished in turn. As one animal eats another, the leaf nutrients are passed from one creature to the next. This process of passing nutrients from animal to animal through feeding is called a *food web*. Food webs exist throughout the world and link together all life on our planet.

brown pelican

Each time leaf particles are passed off as waste, they grow new crops of microbes that nourish particle feeders such as shrimp, clams, snails, and worms. These animals in turn feed fish including snook, tarpon, snapper, and bonefish.

Many insects and land crabs feed on mangrove leaves and digest them. Their waste products help nourish the marine system. By contrast, most marine animals that feed on mangrove leaves don't actually digest them. It is this process that makes the mangrove food web so remarkable: most of the marine animals that consume the leaf particles digest only the microbe coating; the leaf particle passes through the animal intact. A new coating of microbes grows around the particle, and it is eaten again. Once more, only the microbes are digested before the particle is passed out as waste. In this way, each leaf particle is swallowed and eliminated from the body many times by different animals. Each time, a nutritious new coating of microbes grows around it. Thus, each leaf grows many crops of food before it is used up.

Mangroves in Danger

Many mangrove swamps have been destroyed, and many others are in danger. One reason is that people want to use the land for other things. Large areas of swamp are drained and filled in each year so houses and hotels can be built on this "reclaimed" land. Swamps are also dredged to make boat channels and marinas. It is not easy for people to understand the important relationship between mangroves and the abundant marine life in our surrounding seas because this relationship is invisible. By destroying mangrove swamps, we decrease the amount of lobsters, shrimp, snappers, and other seafood available to fishermen; we endanger offshore coral reefs and destroy nesting areas for many birds; we open our coasts to erosion, nutrient loss, and soil depletion.

These tragic effects are not quickly seen or felt, while the benefits of building a hotel or marina are obvious. Yet the damaging effects can be great and far reaching, affecting the quality of life itself.

Destruction

People intentionally destroy mangroves by cutting trees, filling land, building dams, and flooding areas for agriculture and mosquito control projects. People also destroy mangroves unintentionally through carelessness and ignorance, as in the case of oil spills and drifting herbicide sprays.

Flooding programs and oil spills kill mangroves by suffocation. The most vulnerable part of a mangrove tree is its exposed root pores, through which the tree receives oxygen. The pores are designed to keep out water during periods of natural flooding from rainstorms and tides, but if the roots are submerged for too long — as when water is dammed or diked in water management programs — water invades the pores, and the trees die from suffocation. Similarly, oil spills along our coasts can kill entire mangrove swamps by coating and smothering the sensitive roots.

Mangroves are easily poisoned by herbicides and crude oil. Both are absorbed directly through the leaves, injuring or killing the tree. As we use more herbicides in agriculture, and ferry more oil across our oceans, the risk of death from poisoning increases.

The owners of a new home may think nothing of pruning back the red mangroves along their waterfront property to enhance their view, yet even pruning can easily kill red mangroves. Because mangroves are designed to cope with big storms, the amount of swamp destroyed by nature each year is very small compared with the amount destroyed by humans.

The Future

tricolor heron

The death of a mangrove swamp can result in loss of seafood, land erosion, loss of coastal developments and agriculture, death of coral reefs, loss of human lives and wildlife, or all of these combined. It also means the loss of a tree that is used by people for income and to benefit their communities. In some countries, the red mangrove's bark is used to tan leather and as medicine for kidney infection, and its wood is used for cooking, heating, and building. In Florida, black mangrove nectar is used to commercially produce honey. The mangroves' importance to our environment and our safety must be weighed against their usefulness to people. The time when we viewed the earth as a warehouse for our personal use has passed. Today we recognize planet Earth as a living system whose health and welfare must be maintained if we are to survive. Mangrove swamps are an important part of this planetary system.

As people learn more about the importance of mangrove swamps, they are taking steps to protect them. This includes the prevention of dredging and filling mangrove swamps; prevention of permanent flooding or other changes to the natural water flow in the swamp; preventing increased wave action from boat wakes or sea walls; and preventing water pollution from sources such as oil and drifting herbicide sprays. Where mangroves have already been destroyed, new seedlings are planted in reforestation programs. Today, many mangrove areas are protected by law.

Journey's End

raccoon

We have reached the end of our boat journey. Night has fallen, and a raccoon comes to the water's edge to feed on sweet oysters. We watch him reach for an oyster with his tiny black fingers. Just offshore, a great white heron silently stalks a school of small mullet, her keen eyes seeing easily what our human eyes cannot.

In this time of solitude, we quietly reflect on the many roles of the mangrove swamp, some hidden from view yet profoundly significant: a home for wildlife; a protector of our coastal lands and developments; a filter for silt and chemicals that can pollute the ocean and kill coral reefs; a nursery ground for baby marine animals, including commercial ones; an amazing nutrition source for the abundant life in our shallow seas; and in many places, a safeguard for human lives. Yet, every day mangroves are destroyed so people can use the space for homes, for recreation, and for commerce. To developers who see land only as a space for their use, a swamp seems worthless. To commercial fishermen who think of their annual harvest of fish, the same swamp is worth many thousands of dollars and perhaps their way of life. To those who understand the mangrove swamp as an important part of our living planetary system, the swamp is valued as we value the quality of life itself.

great white heron

With understanding comes beauty.
And look, the moon is rising.

www.ingramcontent.com/pod-product-compliance
Lightning Source LLC
Chambersburg PA
CBHW041525070526
44585CB00002B/83